A Letter from the World to America

How the World Sees the USA in 2026

John A. Alexander

**To learn more about John's work, upcoming releases, and
exclusive updates, please visit:**
www.bestsellersbyjohnaalexander.com

For direct contact:
author@bestsellersbyjohnaalexander.com

Published by

Ultra Publishers
www.ultrapublishers.com

Printed in the United States of America

Dedication

As we were writing and completing the last few chapters, we heard that Charlie Kirk was assassinated on September 10th, 2025. He not only touched the USA but also other parts of the world, including us, though we are not Americans. We have followed him for years as he stood for truth and welcomed those who disagreed with him respectfully and with grace.

He was a man of faith, who loved God, and was knowledgeable in many political and social matters that affect our daily lives— marriage, family, and common sense among them. We wept when we heard this terrible news, and our prayers are with his family and all those mourning today.

Thank you, Charlie, for all you did for your country, for the youth, and for those who heard your message around the world. Many will continue your work, perhaps even more powerfully, because of the love people had for you. Thank you.

What Now?

Well, this was the SPARK that ignited a far greater FIRE, one that spread all over the world. What was once intended for evil has become a powerful force for good, a movement that Charlie helped start and that continues to burn brightly. Even though we will miss

Charlie immensely, we can already see what history has shown time and again, that when someone who stands for truth and conviction is silenced, their cause only grows stronger. It happened with many who were unjustly taken from us, and now we see it again in Charlie's case.

Today, hundreds of new chapters of Turning Point are in the process of opening. The movement is expanding beyond anything Charlie himself could have imagined. His voice, once confined to a stage, a microphone, or a podcast, now echoes through countless others who have taken up the same mantle. The voice is louder, the message clearer, and the passion greater than ever before.

The reason for this book is to remind us of the power we hold when we stand for truth, and the courage it takes to do so unashamedly. There is always a price to pay for standing firm in your convictions. The cost is high: you might lose followers, you might be misunderstood, you might even be hated by many, sometimes even by those closest to you. But in the end, we would rather die speaking TRUTH than live comfortably in deception. We would rather be remembered as people of integrity and courage than as those who stayed silent in the face of falsehood.

This book is a call to character, to be the kind of person who loves their country deeply, who seeks to make the world better, and who refuses to compromise truth for approval.

So, how do we make a better world? It begins one person at a time. Influence starts small, with those around you. You may not have the platform to address millions or the privilege of speaking to vast crowds, but you can still change the world by impacting one heart, one life, one moment at a time. Never let fear silence your voice. Never become someone who is too afraid to speak truth when it matters most.

Charlie said it well: *Read as many books as you can every year.* Fill your mind with knowledge so your facts are grounded and your convictions informed. Then share the truth you learn, not with arrogance or hostility, but with boldness, humility, and respect, even toward those who oppose you. That's what Charlie did.

He gave space for people who thought differently. He debated ideas passionately but never stopped loving his country or believing in its promise. He may not have influenced everyone, but he influenced us. So deeply, in fact, that when we heard of his passing, we wept, many of us who had never even met him. He became a HERO to countless people because he lived what so many only talk about doing.

Charlie Kirk showed us what conviction looks like in action. He embodied courage, faith, and truth. And now, it's our turn to carry that forward.

WE ARE CHARLIE KIRK!

Acknowledgment

Messengers of Truth: The Courage to Speak.

In every generation, there are voices that refuse to be silenced—truth-tellers who challenge the status quo, confront injustice, and awaken the conscience of society. Messengers of Truth honors these history makers: bold individuals who speak not for applause, but for impact.

They are poets, prophets, journalists, reformers, and everyday citizens who risk comfort for clarity, popularity for principle. Their words ignite movements. Their truths reshape nations. Their legacy is not merely what they said, but what they dared to say when silence would have been safer.

This book is a tribute to those who speak truth even when it costs them everything. May their stories stir your spirit, strengthen your resolve, sharpen your voice, and remind you that history is shaped by those who refuse to whisper when the world needs a roar.

"IT IS NOT WHAT WE ARE AGAINST, BUT WHAT WE ARE FOR. WE ARE FOR TRUTH."

About the Author

John has traveled extensively around the world, teaching and speaking to companies and religious organizations on topics that remain deeply relevant today. His lectures span a wide range of subjects—from business and politics to personal development, sales, leadership, and marriage—all with a consistent purpose: to challenge his audience to think critically, grow confidently, and strive to become better individuals in every area of life.

With more than forty years of experience influencing and inspiring people face-to-face, John is now embracing a lifelong passion—writing. Through his books, he seeks to share the lessons, insights, and wisdom he has gained over decades of teaching, leadership, and global experience.

He plans to publish four to five books each year, ensuring this is only the beginning of what readers can expect from him. John's knowledge is profound, thought-provoking, and always grounded in truth.

Table of Contents

Introduction..i

Chapter 1 When Officials Get Sworn Into Office 1

Chapter 2 Our View on Democrats.. 4

Chapter 3 Future Elections Result... 9

Chapter 4 The Supreme Court of the USA 14

Chapter 5 Officials, Judges, Protecting Illegal Immigrants 19

Chapter 6 Abraham Lincoln Proclaims a Fasr and Prayer 24

Chapter 7 Our View on Republicans.. 28

Chapter 8 The Trump Deranged Syndrome.. 33

Chapter 9 The Mystery of Who is Funding Antifa? 39

Chapter 10 Israel, Iran, Hamas, Russia and Others............................ 42

Chapter 11 The Goal for Open Borders (To Get Votes)................... 46

Chapter 12 A Call to So-Called Christians, Believers, and Religious 49

Chapter 13 The Insanity of Santuary Cities 52

Chapter 14 A Word to the Stream Media: Power of Media to Deceive
.... 56

Chapter 15 Creating a Department to Handle Fact Checking (Fact Check Government Department) 59

Chapter 16 "False Rhetoric" Leads to Violence 62

Chapter 17 Democrats Seem Like They're from Another Planet: Supporting Illegal 65

Chapter 18 Criminals Released from Prison to Murder Someone 68

Chapter 19 The Left and Far Left Never Thought Trump Would Have the Power House Again 71

Chapter 20 The Insanity of Tapping Officials' Phones 75

Chapter 21 Socialism/Communism 78

Chapter 22 The Children 81

Introduction

The purpose of this book is to share how the world perceives what has been happening in the United States, regarding presidents, policies, borders, and how democratic nations view these developments.

There is a saying: *"An outsider can see better; an outsider can see the blind spots; there are three sides to every story."*

Over the years, the world has observed two dominant perspectives within the United States: the Republican and the Democrat viewpoints, and now we see the far left point of view. The goal of this book is to offer readers in the U.S. an opportunity to see how outsiders interpret America's challenges and to share what the international community might view as possible solutions.

Every nation desires to be great, prosperous, and safe. Yet this has not always been the case, even for powerful nations like the United States. If our grandparents or great-grandparents could see the state of the world today, they might be surprised by how much has changed, how values once considered foundational or moral have become increasingly debated or redefined.

What our children are exposed to, what parents allow, what is being taught in schools, and the political motives behind open-border policies, all these shape the moral and social fabric of a nation. When justice fails or when repeat offenders go unpunished, societies risk endangering their future generations. Political decisions made for short-term gain can have long-term consequences for an entire people.

Some are blinded by ideology or influenced by corruption, allowing harmful policies to persist. Yet, if societies wish to preserve their values and freedoms, they must act with wisdom and urgency because division and moral decay can spread rapidly. *"It is now or never."*

For centuries, nations have resisted the spread of socialism and communism, understanding the devastation these systems have brought throughout history. Yet today, some movements within democratic societies seem to embrace elements of these ideologies. The danger is that political parties, once defenders of liberty, sometimes support policies that contradict those very principles. Citizens must remain alert to ensure freedom is not lost through complacency or deception.

As the saying goes, *"Let us not complain about things we have allowed."* Those who live under authoritarian regimes can testify that they were deceived by false promises. They now bear the consequences of those choices, while others still demand the same path.

Throughout this book, each chapter will highlight how we, as individuals, parents, and leaders, must protect the next generation. The true threat to any democracy is not one political party but the erosion of shared values and the loss of moral conviction. When faith, ethics, and truth are undermined, nations grow weaker. Many believe that forces opposed to those values seek to remove God and moral foundations from society, leaving future generations without direction or hope.

The world our children will inherit may differ greatly from the one we grew up in. Yet even in dark times, grace and goodness can prevail. This generation must nurture faith, integrity, sound education, and character. We must prepare our children to face challenges with courage and to fight for what is right, not out of hate, but out of love for truth and freedom.

The United States has long understood the power of prayer. This may be another defining moment to pray for the nation and its future. History records how President Abraham Lincoln once called citizens to fasting and prayer, and the nation experienced a moral renewal. Looking back helps us see how far we have come, and how far we may have strayed. Let us rise, as people across the world, to stand for truth before it is too late. *Lord, help us, we pray.*

CHAPTER 1
WHEN OFFICIALS GET SWORN INTO OFFICE

In the United States, politicians take an oath that varies depending on their office, but all require them to swear or affirm their commitment to upholding the Constitution and performing their duties faithfully.

For the President, the oath is specified in the Constitution and reads:

"I do solemnly swear (or affirm) that I will faithfully execute the Office of President of the United States, and will, to the best of my ability, preserve, protect, and defend the Constitution of the United States."

For others holding office in the government, the oath is as follows:

"I do solemnly swear (or affirm) that I will support and defend the Constitution of the United States against all enemies, foreign and domestic; that I will bear true faith and allegiance to the same; that I take this obligation freely, without any mental reservation or purpose of evasion; and that I will well and faithfully discharge the duties of the office on which I am about to enter. So help me God."

The concern many around the world observe is that political partisanship can sometimes overshadow this solemn promise. When loyalty to party or power takes precedence over duty to country, it undermines public trust and the Constitution itself.

In recent years, some leaders have been perceived as allowing or overlooking actions that appear to weaken national integrity, often for political advantage. To many outsiders, this seems like a betrayal of public service in favor of self-interest.

In some nations, officials who act against the national interest face serious legal consequences. Thus, it can be difficult for observers abroad to understand why certain U.S. officials seem to tolerate practices that appear to contradict federal law—such as the designation of "Sanctuary Cities." The question often raised is: *If it is illegal to harbor criminals, why are such policies allowed to continue?*

The United States has strong institutions, Homeland Security, the Department of Justice, the Supreme Court, all meant to uphold justice and protect its citizens. Yet some leaders appear to challenge or reinterpret these responsibilities.

A balanced approach to immigration and law enforcement is essential. Those who entered the United States illegally in recent years should face enforcement under current laws. At the same time, individuals who came long ago and have contributed meaningfully to society could be considered for legal pathways. Ultimately, this is a policy decision for the sitting administration, but fairness and humanity should guide it.

Finally, ensuring accountability among politicians who act against the nation's best interests would send a vital message: that public office exists to serve the people, not the party, and certainly not personal ambition.

Chapter 2
Our View on Democrats

How most (majority) of the world sees the Democrats in the USA?

Over the past several years, the political landscape of the United States has been closely watched by the global community. The world observes not only America's policies but also the conduct and intentions of its two dominant parties: the Democratic Party and the Republican Party. The image of these parties abroad has fluctuated dramatically, especially following major events such as elections, foreign policy shifts, and domestic social movements. Many nations view American politics as a reflection of broader Western ideological struggles, between tradition and progressivism, capitalism and socialism, sovereignty and globalism.

In the past few years, we witnessed the true nature of the two dominant parties in the USA: the Democrats and the Republicans. The Republicans accomplished significant progress from 2016–2020, which was seen as positive. In contrast, the Democratic Party began revealing its agenda without regard for consequences, exposing schemes to undermine opponents. By 2025, much of their strategy had been revealed and failed.

This period became a turning point in global perception. While Republicans were often viewed as focusing on strengthening national interests, economic independence, and border control, the Democrats were increasingly seen as leaning toward ideological extremism. Many foreign observers, from Europe to Asia, Africa, and South America, began questioning the motives behind Democratic policies that appeared to prioritize political power and social control over practical governance.

Why didn't it work for the Democrats? Because their actions and lies were exposed to the world.

For many around the globe, this exposure was not just political theater but a revelation of deeper systemic issues. International media outlets, independent journalists, and analysts began to dissect the contradictions within Democratic rhetoric, speaking of equality while supporting policies that deepened division, or promising transparency while evidence of corruption and censorship surfaced.

Many believe the 2020 election was stolen. From our perspective, this exposure was necessary for the world to see the true agenda of the Democrats—prioritizing votes over the nation's welfare. Their blind pursuit of power disregarded the future of their children, highlighting a dangerous blind spot unnoticed by them but obvious to the world.

Global audiences watched the unfolding events surrounding the 2020 election with disbelief. Regardless of where one stands politically, there was an undeniable sense of mistrust that spread across international borders. Many saw the Democratic Party's strategies as desperate attempts to consolidate influence, often at the expense of truth, unity, and moral leadership. The narrative of "vote at all costs" created an image of a party detached from reality, unwilling to confront its own contradictions.

The world observed the performance of both parties: 2016–2020 for Republicans and 2020–2024 for Democrats. The Democrats' actions that drew international criticism included:

- Open borders prioritized political gain over national security.
- Thousands of children entered the country unaccompanied, risking exploitation and abuse.
- Education was undermined through inappropriate materials and speakers in schools; no Democrats opposed this, nor did they oppose open borders, though they criticized Republicans attempting reforms.
- Policies and intentions for 2025–2026 remain unclear, while many Democrats embrace socialism and communism, threatening the country's future.
- Corruption has been widespread, with billions of dollars mismanaged or redirected for personal gain by government officials.

- Governors and mayors hinder law enforcement and protect criminals, prioritizing political agendas over public safety.

- Politicians abusing power remain protected temporarily by law until evidence allows for prosecution. Uninformed voters inadvertently sustain this system.

- Hatred for one individual has blinded many Democrats, risking historical condemnation.

- Some Democrats still have the chance to return to common sense, uphold true democracy, and serve the nation effectively.

These points have been echoed not only by political critics but also by concerned citizens and leaders across the world who once viewed the United States as a beacon of stability. Many foreign governments have quietly expressed concern about the moral and ethical decline they perceive in America's political class, a decline amplified by partisanship, censorship, and media manipulation.

Observers from abroad also note that the Democratic Party's growing alignment with socialist ideologies mirrors patterns seen in collapsing regimes throughout history. When a ruling party prioritizes ideological purity over pragmatic problem-solving, societies often face economic instability, social unrest, and moral confusion.

Despite the criticism, hope remains. The world recognizes that within the Democratic Party there are still individuals of integrity, those willing to challenge corruption, defend constitutional principles, and restore balance to governance. These members could play a pivotal role in reshaping the party's direction, steering it away from extremism and back toward genuine public service.

Ultimately, the global perception of the Democrats is not fixed. It is shaped continuously by their actions, accountability, and willingness to learn from past mistakes. The coming years, particularly 2025–2026, will determine whether the Democratic Party chooses reform and transparency or continues down a path that alienates both Americans and international allies.

If the Democrats can rediscover the values of honesty, respect for law, and true democratic dialogue, the world might yet regain confidence in them. But if they persist in prioritizing control over service, division over unity, and ideology over truth, their global reputation may continue to decline, leaving a legacy of lost trust and missed opportunity.

CHAPTER 3
FUTURE ELECTIONS RESULT

As the United States moves deeper into the 2020s, political analysts, citizens, and international observers are all asking the same question: *What direction will America take next?* The last decade has been one of extraordinary turbulence, marked by global crises, domestic unrest, and rapid shifts in voter priorities. Against this backdrop, the Republican and Democratic parties continue to represent two distinct visions for the country's future.

From an international standpoint, it appears that the Republican Party has successfully positioned itself as the party of structure, accountability, and national identity, while the Democratic Party faces internal fragmentation and a crisis of public confidence. Economic concerns, border security, and moral integrity have become the defining issues of the era, and these factors are shaping electoral outcomes across state and federal levels.

The way we see it, Republicans are likely to maintain power through 2032. If Republicans continue to focus on policy and action as promised to voters, Democrats have little chance of winning in 2026 or 2028. Republicans will likely strengthen their control of the Senate, House, and White House.

This projection is not based solely on partisanship but on measurable performance indicators. The Republican platform, focused on lowering inflation, reinforcing law and order, re-establishing energy independence, and protecting constitutional freedoms, resonates deeply with middle-class Americans. Voters have grown weary of divisive rhetoric and symbolic gestures; they increasingly demand tangible results.

If Republicans maintain a disciplined agenda emphasizing economic recovery, job creation, and national security, they are positioned to dominate the political landscape well into the next decade. Key battleground states—once considered reliably blue—are showing signs of shifting as independent voters and moderates distance themselves from the perceived excesses of Democratic leadership.

Democrats need to stop attacking every Republican move, elect a credible leader, and return to pro-USA policies. A fair election requires addressing issues like illegal immigration, law enforcement, and corruption. Currently, Democrats appear cornered and continue to attack opponents, inadvertently strengthening Republican positions.

Many political observers agree that the Democrats' current strategy—defined by opposition rather than innovation—has backfired. The continuous focus on discrediting Republican figures instead of offering viable solutions has alienated both centrist voters and international allies. To regain footing, the Democratic Party must shift from reactionary tactics toward proactive, patriotic leadership. Without a unifying message or charismatic leader who can inspire broad confidence, the party risks further decline in voter turnout and fundraising power.

Steps for Democrats to regain credibility:

1. **Acknowledge and support positive Republican initiatives to gain trust.**

Voters respect humility and cooperation. Recognizing effective Republican policies—especially those that benefit all Americans—could demonstrate maturity and a renewed commitment to bipartisan progress.

2. **Admit that open borders harmed the country and commit to secure borders.**

Security is not a partisan issue. By acknowledging the consequences of weak immigration enforcement, Democrats could rebuild credibility with suburban and working-class communities that have suffered from the resulting social and economic strain.

3. **Support legal pathways for long-term residents and cooperate with deportation of illegal entrants involved in crime.**

A balanced immigration policy would show both compassion and firmness, distinguishing lawful immigrants from those who exploit the system. This balance could win back moderate voters seeking fairness without extremism.

4. **Work with ICE to return criminals to their home countries, especially those who entered during open borders.**

Public safety must come before political correctness. Cooperation with immigration enforcement would signal that Democrats prioritize citizens' well-being over ideological narratives.

5. **Reject policies allowing men in women's sports, women's bathrooms, and women's prisons.**

Cultural issues have become flashpoints that define modern politics. By returning to biological and traditional standards of fairness, Democrats could re-engage voters who have felt alienated by radical social experiments.

6. **Protect children affected by previous open-border policies. Prioritize safety and lawful status to gain trust from the public.**

Protecting vulnerable children, both American-born and immigrant, should be a universal priority. Restoring integrity to the immigration system and ensuring child welfare could help heal divisions and rebuild public confidence.

Failing to implement these measures risks long-term damage to Democratic cities and the party itself. Our hope is that Democrats will carefully consider these steps, prioritize national welfare, and restore trust with voters.

If these corrections are ignored, the long-term outcome appears predictable: Democratic influence will continue to shrink to urban centers already burdened by crime, homelessness, and economic stagnation. Meanwhile, Republican states—often characterized by stronger economies, lower taxes, and higher public safety—will serve as the model for national renewal.

Ultimately, the next several election cycles will determine not just who governs, but what kind of country the United States will become. If Democrats reform themselves and embrace genuine patriotism, America may once again experience balanced governance. However, if they persist in polarization and ideological rigidity, the electorate will likely continue to favor Republican leadership— potentially shaping U.S. politics through 2032 and beyond.

CHAPTER 4
THE SUPREME COURT OF THE USA

Our observation here is very delicate. Comments from both parties have divided the country and affected the credibility of the Supreme Court. Many argue there are so many Democrats and Republicans on the Supreme Court, which is incorrect. Justices are there to uphold the Constitution, not personal opinions, and to make decisions in the best interest of the citizens and the nation.

A judge once said that upon entering the chambers, they are not blue or red, but black robes representing the Constitution and the people. They must navigate these challenges while considering their families and the impact on future generations.

In every great republic, there exists a cornerstone institution designed to safeguard liberty, maintain balance, and ensure that no branch of government exceeds its authority. In the United States, that institution is the Supreme Court. The Supreme Court holds the sacred duty of interpreting and upholding the Constitution, not for the benefit of a party or ideology, but for the protection and stability of the people.

However, as the world observes the current state of American governance, serious concerns have emerged about how far the judiciary has drifted from its constitutional purpose. Judicial activism, political favoritism, and ideological manipulation now threaten to erode public confidence in what was once considered the most respected branch of government.

If the Supreme Court has the power of the Constitution, they **MUST** back up things that are for the best of the citizens and stop all the nonsense going on. Far-left judges abusing their powers to stop the progress of securing an open border, of deporting illegals back to their countries, the world sees these things taking place and makes every institution of law and order a joke when they allow these things to take place. The way we see it, that this nonsense can enter the Supreme Court judges and affect the decisions they make, and it is very clear that the left most of the time votes one way, and the right votes differently. That should NOT be; it should be to uphold the Constitution and protect the citizens of the USA, rather than to allow politics to influence the decisions made.

The judiciary must remember that its loyalty lies not to party, but to the principles of justice and the Constitution. When judicial rulings are driven by ideology instead of evidence, or when political loyalty supersedes national duty, the entire legal system begins to crumble from within. The world notices this erosion of integrity. Nations that once looked to America as a model of justice now question whether its institutions can still stand above corruption and bias.

The Democrats, after they lost the House and Senate, if you remember, the first thing they said by their leader at the time was, "Let us place our judges everywhere." Their goal is to place left-leaning judges in order to stop what the opposition wants to do, and we have seen it and continue to see it.

This strategy, widely acknowledged even by independent analysts, reflects a deliberate attempt to use the courts as political weapons rather than instruments of impartial justice. Instead of respecting the separation of powers, the practice of stacking courts with ideological loyalists has weakened trust in judicial rulings and undermined the fairness that democracy depends on. When the courts become extensions of political campaigns, the people lose faith in the very idea of justice.

If a governor or a mayor of a city fails to protect their citizens and doesn't agree in adding more law enforcement to their cities, and announces in **PUBLIC** that they do **NOT** want help with the crime in their cities, and fights ICE or any law enforcement that is trying to come in and do the job that their governors and mayors should be doing, they should be removed from office and they should go to prison for putting the votes of illegals before U.S. citizens.

The actions of the Democrats are very clear to the world. As mentioned, an outsider can see the blind spots better; indeed, these politicians are blind to think that the world doesn't see their corruption and how they protect illegals to get their votes. They provide them with healthcare, money, food, and driver's licenses, especially without passing a driver's course to operate those huge trucks. The world sees it, and the worst part is that no immediate action is taken to enforce the law. Yet they all cry "due process."

What is the due process for someone who came illegally to a country? Simple: proof of entering the country illegally is all that is needed. Then the process is to get them back to their country or take advantage of the offer to self-deport.

This approach is neither cruel nor unjust, it is a matter of national sovereignty. Every country has the right to defend its borders and to regulate who may enter or remain within its territory. America must do the same, not out of hatred, but out of love for the rule of law and for the safety of its own citizens.

Please, **Supreme** Court **of the** United States **judges**, use your powers, and the powers of the Constitution, to protect the citizens of your country. Stop these far-left judges from giving all judges a terrible name, as the world watches in disgust. **AMERICA FIRST** must be your goal: not party, but your **country** and the **citizens** who depend on you to uphold justice.

If every nation on Earth placed its own country and its citizens first, the world would be far more stable and peaceful. When leaders protect their people, enforce their laws, and preserve their sovereignty, mutual respect among nations follows naturally. America's example matters, and the Supreme Court's courage in defending its Constitution will define not just the future of the United States, but the integrity of justice worldwide.

CHAPTER 5
OFFICIALS, JUDGES, PROTECTING ILLEGAL IMMIGRANTS

Around the world, people look to the United States as a symbol of justice, integrity, and leadership. Yet in recent years, that reputation has been challenged. Many foreign observers are left questioning how government officials, judges, and elected representatives—those sworn to defend the Constitution and protect their citizens—can act in ways that appear to contradict the very principles they vowed to uphold.

This is one issue the world doesn't understand: how can government officials, including judges, act against the best interests of the people who elected them?

The answer, as seen by many inside and outside the nation, lies in the dangerous rise of political justice, a system in which decisions are no longer based on law or fact, but on ideology and personal allegiance. The result is a deep fracture within America's institutions of power, eroding public confidence and diminishing the moral authority of the judiciary.

Political Judges

After the Republican victory on November 5th, 2024, Chuck Schumer announced plans to appoint liberal judges to block the new President's initiatives. Many viewed this as prioritizing party over country. The world sees this as corruption and abuse of office.

Such statements, coming from senior political figures, confirmed what many had long suspected that the courts are being used not to uphold justice, but to obstruct legitimate governance. Around the globe, nations that once looked to the U.S. for examples of balanced democracy now see its legal system as increasingly partisan, where political loyalty overrides judicial neutrality.

Actions include:

- Judges delaying or blocking presidential actions for political purposes. Accountability laws should be enforced to prevent this.
- Congress must stop judges from making political decisions, ensuring they defend the Constitution fairly.
- Judges releasing criminals who then commit serious crimes, harming citizens. Congress and the Supreme Court must act to prevent these injustices.
- Protecting illegal immigrants over law-abiding citizens. Judges violating the law should be removed, charged, and held accountable.

- Senators defending illegal immigrants and undermining law enforcement are contributing to threats against the USA. They must be removed from office.

Each of these actions reflects a larger failure of responsibility. When those in positions of power protect lawbreakers while punishing those who enforce the law, a dangerous precedent is set. It signals to criminals and foreign actors alike that the nation's laws can be manipulated or ignored.

In many cases, decisions made under the banner of "human rights" or "social justice" have instead endangered innocent citizens. When courts order the release of violent offenders or block deportations of individuals with criminal histories, communities suffer the consequences. Families lose loved ones, law enforcement officers lose morale, and trust in government fades.

Furthermore, judges and officials who protect illegal immigrants at the expense of citizens are not showing compassion—they are undermining justice. Every sovereign nation has the right and obligation to determine who may enter its borders and under what conditions. When that principle is violated, national security weakens, and so does respect for the rule of law.

Congress and the Supreme Court have both a moral and constitutional duty to correct these abuses. The enforcement of judicial accountability should not be viewed as an attack on independence, but as a defense of integrity. Judges are not above the law; they are entrusted with it. When they use their positions for political advantage, they betray not only the people but also the very Constitution they swore to uphold.

Restoring Accountability

Rebuilding faith in the justice system begins with holding officials and judges accountable for their actions. Mechanisms such as judicial review, impeachment, and oversight committees must be strengthened and used without hesitation when misconduct occurs. Political favoritism in the courtroom is a threat as grave as corruption in any other branch of government.

At the same time, lawmakers must prioritize citizen safety over political agendas. Sanctuary policies that shield illegal immigrants from deportation may seem compassionate in theory, but they have resulted in increased crime rates, drug trafficking, and exploitation of vulnerable individuals. Protecting the American people should be non-negotiable, and any official or judge who obstructs that responsibility must answer for their actions.

The United States cannot afford to normalize lawlessness within its own government. Every nation's stability begins with respect for its laws. When judges manipulate rulings for political gain, or when senators defend illegal behavior for electoral advantage, the very foundation of democracy is shaken.

The USA must pray for leadership that protects citizens and future generations.

True leadership does not fear accountability; it welcomes it. The world is watching America closely, hoping to see a return to justice grounded in truth, not politics. The time has come for every official, from the highest judge to the smallest local leader, to remember their oath, restore integrity to public office, and once again make the phrase "equal justice under law" mean something real.

If America reclaims this moral clarity, it will not only heal its internal divisions but also restore its standing as a global example of fairness, strength, and freedom.

CHAPTER 6
ABRAHAM LINCOLN PROCLAIMS A FAST AND PRAYER

Abraham Lincoln proclaimed a day of national humiliation, fasting, and prayer on April 30, 1863. The proclamation emphasized confessing national sins, seeking mercy, and relying on divine guidance for the nation's restoration.

Imagine implementing such a day today, perhaps annually before elections, for Americans to fast, pray, and seek repentance. Historically, the USA embraced God as central to its identity, reflected on currency and in cultural practices. Respect for faith and morality was foundational to the nation's success.

Heres is a copy of the declaration of Abraham Lincoln for a day of "Humiliation, a day to fast and pray."

A Proclamation

Whereas the Senate of the United States, devoutly recognizing the supreme authority and just government of Almighty God in all the affairs of men and of nations, has by a resolution requested the President to designate and set apart a day for national prayer and humiliation; and

Whereas it is the duty of nations as well as of men to own their dependence upon the overruling power of God, to confess their sins and transgressions in humble sorrow, yet with assured hope that genuine repentance will lead to mercy and pardon, and to recognize the sublime truth, announced in the Holy Scriptures and proven by all history, that those nations only are blessed whose God is the Lord;

And, insomuch as we know that by His divine law nations, like individuals, are subjected to punishments and chastisements in this world, may we not justly fear that the awful calamity of civil war which now desolates the land may be but a punishment inflicted upon us for our presumptuous sins, to the needful end of our national reformation as a whole people? We have been the recipients of the choicest bounties of Heaven; we have been preserved these many years in peace and prosperity; we have grown in numbers, wealth, and power as no other nation has ever grown. But we have forgotten God. We have forgotten the gracious hand which preserved us in peace and multiplied and enriched and strengthened us, and we have vainly imagined, in the deceitfulness of our hearts, that all these blessings were produced by some superior wisdom and virtue of our own. Intoxicated with unbroken success, we have become too self-sufficient to feel the necessity of redeeming and preserving grace, too proud to pray to the God that made us.

It behooves us, then, to humble ourselves before the offended Power, to confess our national sins, and to pray for clemency and forgiveness.

Now, therefore, in compliance with the request, and fully concurring in the views of the Senate, I do by this my proclamation designate and set apart Thursday, the 30th day of April, 1863, as a day of national humiliation, fasting, and prayer. And I do hereby request all the people to abstain on that day from their ordinary secular pursuits, and to unite at their several places of public worship and their respective homes in keeping the day holy to the Lord and devoted to the humble discharge of the religious duties proper to that solemn occasion.

All this being done in sincerity and truth, let us then rest humbly in the hope authorized by the divine teachings that the united cry of the nation will be heard on high and answered with blessings no less than the pardon of our national sins and the restoration of our now divided and suffering country to its former happy condition of unity and peace. In witness whereof I have hereunto set my hand and caused the seal of the United States to be affixed.

Done at the city of Washington, this 30th day of March, A. D. 1863, and of the Independence of the United States the eighty-seventh.

ABRAHAM LINCOLN

By the President:

WILLIAM H. SEWARD, Secretary of State.

Is taken from the "The American Presidency Project" and given credit to

https://www.presidency.ucsb.edu/documents/proclamation-97-appointing-day-national-humiliation-fasting-and-prayer

CHAPTER 7
OUR VIEW ON REPUBLICANS

$\mathcal{E}$ven with a Republican majority in the House and Senate, some Republicans vote against party policies, undermining unity. This weakens the party's credibility and frustrates observers internationally. Leaders must align with party and public interest while voicing concerns internally before voting.

The USA is showing progress and gaining respect globally. Central America is seeing success in crime reduction and reform, which serves as an example. Citizens, regardless of political affiliation, should be proud of the country's advancements. Those prioritizing party over national welfare risk being considered traitors to the country.

THE IMPORTANCE OF UNITY AND STRONG LEADERSHIP

A nation's strength is built upon the unity of its people and the integrity of those chosen to represent them. In a time when political division seems to define every debate, it is vital for elected officials to remember the higher purpose of public service: to protect, to strengthen, and to unify. The world is watching how America manages its internal conflicts, and it judges not just by words, but by actions.

If **98% of your party** stands one way and you don't agree on some things, then meet with your party and share your concerns. You might get a deal or not—if you get a deal, great, but if you don't, you must show your party and those you represent that **unity of party is a priority**, remembering that it is probably the President who gave you the opportunity for the office you hold—especially with a sitting President who fought for the country and for the people you represent. Those voters supported him, not you.

Party unity is not blind loyalty; it is disciplined cooperation for the greater good. A divided party weakens the nation and emboldens those who thrive on chaos. True leadership requires humility, the ability to compromise when possible, and the wisdom to stand together when national security and moral order are at stake.

Of course, if **50% of the party** is against something, then the party has a duty to hear their concerns and seek unity—that is **democracy**. But to oppose because you simply do not like the President, or because of personal ambition or pride, would be worse than the worst betrayal. Leaders must rise above personal feelings and remember that they were chosen to serve, not to divide.

The world sees more **positive than negative** in what your administration has done, and many nations would love to have such leadership. Even here, in our country, we recognize the good that comes from a party determined to do what is right for its people. Strong, decisive leadership often faces fierce opposition—not because it fails, but because it succeeds.

Strong Leadership Matters

STRONG LEADERSHIP will shake corruption from the top and stir many feathers. But that is the mark of genuine reform. When a leader is firm in purpose, corruption trembles, and those who have benefited from disorder will always resist. Remember, strong leadership **will protect our children**, will protect our nations, and will guard our values from those who seek to destroy them.

Evil will always try to fight everything strong leadership accomplishes, because it threatens to undo the damage caused by weak or self-serving leadership. History teaches that moral clarity and firm decision-making are always met with resistance, yet they are the only path toward lasting stability and prosperity.

Republicans, be proud of your party and stand as the best party the USA has ever had, or be counted among those who opposed what was best for your country. This is not the time for hesitation or internal sabotage. It is the time to stand firm, united, and unwavering in defense of American values and the Constitution.

Leadership and Moral Integrity

Remember that the **previous administration** will go down in history as one of the worst, not only for its policies but for what it allowed to happen in the heart of the nation's capital. What shocked the world most was what took place at the **White House**, where a woman publicly exposed herself for the world to see. That act was more than indecent; it symbolized the moral decline and disrespect that had taken root.

If that is what some voted for, they should feel ashamed for endorsing such a display. Leadership must set a standard worthy of respect—not promote vulgarity or lawlessness under the guise of freedom. Nations fall when moral decay is celebrated and when leaders fail to lead by example.

We are not required to **love or** even **like our leaders**, but we are called to **pray for them**. Through prayer, discernment grows; through humility, understanding deepens; and through faith, nations find their way back to righteousness.

A Call to Faith and Clarity

In times of division and deception, prayer is not weakness, it is strength. It opens the heart to truth and aligns the will with what is just. America, like every great nation, must rediscover this truth: that leadership without morality leads to destruction, but leadership guided by faith and unity leads to restoration.

The world yearns for America to be strong again, united, principled, and fearless in defense of truth. Let every citizen, judge, governor, and representative remember that their actions reflect not just on themselves, but on the soul of the nation they serve.

Be blessed, and may wisdom guide those who lead, courage strengthen those who serve, and faith restore the heart of America.

CHAPTER 8
THE TRUMP DERANGED
SYNDROME

This is the biggest downfall of the Democrats. Republicans are taking advantage of it while Democrats have fallen into the trap. Many Democrats reject anything associated with Trump, showing the public they prioritize party over country. This is not a sustainable strategy.

Republicans are fueling this divide and benefitting politically. Democrats' obsession with opposing Trump is costing them credibility and influence. Unless they refocus on policies that help citizens, not illegal immigrants, they risk further decline in 2026 and 2028. Their hatred for one man has clouded judgment and blinded them to what truly matters.

We praise the few Democrats standing up to this mindset. They show maturity by recognizing good policies regardless of who proposes them. Such balance demonstrates care for the country's future.

The world sees Democrats embracing socialism and communism—systems that have destroyed nations. Many have been deceived by media manipulation and false promises. Even some religious leaders support ideologies that contradict their beliefs, voting for policies that harm their communities and children.

Democrats must return to common sense and reject the extreme ideas that have tarnished their image. The White House flying both the American and LGBTQ flags symbolized a moral decline when public indecency was tolerated without condemnation. This behavior humiliated the nation before the world.

If there is a God—and we believe in a Holy God—these acts will have consequences. Corruption will continue to be exposed, and accountability will come. This is not political judgment but divine correction. We are living in a season of mercy; people and nations must return to faith and righteousness. The call is clear: **Wake up and get ready.**

Around the world, leadership is measured not by popularity or political gamesmanship but by courage, conviction, and moral clarity. When leaders abandon their principles for fear of party backlash, they cease to be representatives of the people and become mere instruments of power. Sadly, this is what many observers now see happening within the Democratic Party of the United States.

Sad to see Democrats as puppets of their party, with the exception of a few brave ones. It is sad because we know that the reason they are afraid to do what is right is because they fear the consequences they might receive. That is not true leadership or strong leadership; that is caving in to the wrong and looking terrible in front of the people you are supposed to represent. The world sees **WEAK** and **CORRUPT** leadership, but it is never too late to be a strong leader for the nation and the people you represent. This is how the world sees you, and probably 80% of your country.

The tragedy of modern politics is that many officials, particularly within the Democratic ranks, no longer act out of conviction but out of fear. Fear of losing influence. Fear of being criticized. Fear of being ostracized by their peers. Yet the world recognizes that real leadership begins when fear ends. A true leader stands firm for truth and justice even when it costs them something, especially when it costs them something.

The only way we see the Democrats winning an election is by talking about what they can do for the people of their nation, rather than fighting for illegals and fighting law enforcement that are doing their job to clean up the streets of your nation. But truthfully, we do not see a change; we believe that they will continue their rhetoric language, and the Republicans will enjoy many years of government because of it.

This is a point many in the international community also echo. The Democratic Party's focus on defending illegal immigration, weakening law enforcement, and embracing divisive ideologies has alienated countless citizens who simply want safety, prosperity, and stability. Instead of constructive solutions, they offer criticism, obstruction, and endless outrage. And in doing so, they push even moderate Americans toward the Republican side, a party increasingly seen as the voice of order and reason in a time of chaos.

Leadership Requires Maturity

It is sad to see politicians behave as children and think the world sees them as adults. In other words, they need to mature and grow up in order to win elections. You can win, but your hate for one person must be put away, and you must **praise the good** that their administration is doing. When you do this, you will see your numbers go up.

But when you endorse socialism, thinking that it is the answer for the future of the party and the country, you are deceiving yourselves. To the world, it is a sign of **desperation** and **last resort**, hoping that you will hit a home run, but all you are doing is fooling yourselves. These words are not meant as condemnation but as a call to reflection. A political party that cannot self-correct will eventually self-destruct. History is filled with examples of movements that collapsed because their leaders cared more about ideology than people, more about optics than outcomes. When power becomes the goal rather than service, decay always follows.

The World is Watching

From abroad, observers continue to express confusion and disappointment. America was once the global symbol of unity through diversity, strength through conviction, and justice through principle. Now, many see a nation divided by petty partisanship and blinded by emotion. Even allies shake their heads as they watch American politicians act not as statesmen but as rivals in an endless contest of insults and vengeance.

Democrats, particularly those in positions of influence, have a choice to make. They can continue on this path of internal decay—serving the loudest voices and the most radical factions—or they can rediscover the foundational principles that once made their party respected: defending working families, protecting the nation, and promoting fairness through law and order.

The world doesn't want to see America fail. On the contrary, nations across the globe hope to see a revival of true American leadership, leadership that is strong, honest, and unafraid to do what is right, even when it is unpopular.

It is never too late to turn back from the wrong path. The courage to change direction is what separates weak leaders from great ones. Those within the Democratic Party who still have integrity, who still remember what public service truly means, must rise up, speak out, and lead by example.

Do not let fear silence you. Do not let corruption define you. Do not let hatred for one man destroy your vision for an entire nation. Step forward, seek unity, and work for the good of all Americans, not just for political advantage.

Because when the dust settles, history will not remember who shouted the loudest, it will remember who stood for what was right.

Be strong, be wise, and above all, be leaders worthy of the people you represent.

CHAPTER 9
THE MYSTERY OF WHO IS FUNDING ANTIFA?

The question many are asking is: who is funding Antifa?
The answer is clear—it is not conservatives. The funding likely comes from far-left domestic and international sources aiming to destabilize the USA.

Their objective is to weaken the nation. Although the current administration is working to counter these threats, stronger action is needed. Internal conflict must be confronted with the same intensity as foreign wars.

Every federal official takes an oath to defend the Constitution against all enemies, foreign and domestic. Many have forgotten this sacred duty. The failure to enforce these principles allows subversive groups to thrive.

The funding of Antifa is likely tied to socialist or communist regimes that oppose American values. Eventually, investigations by agencies like the FBI will expose these entities and their backers.

We commend the current administration for efforts to restore safety and order. The USA's focus on protecting its citizens and securing the nation sets an example for others worldwide.

We know that all these sources funding these protests will eventually come to the open, and many will go to prison for it and their pawns receiving payments for their acts of violence and protests. The world knows it is well organized and probably well-funded, but they have a huge obstacle before them: strong leadership, a very strong administration. We can see that they are united in one cause, and that is what makes them strong and confident—because they want to undo the wrong of a nation and want the best for their citizens and the next generations to come.

This kind of unity and determination, though often found in misguided causes, reminds us how powerful a single purpose can be when people move together with one heart and one mind. When good people, guided by moral conviction and genuine love for their nation, stand together with shared purpose, no opposition can easily break them. That is why strong leadership rooted in integrity and truth is so critical—it becomes the immovable wall that protects a people's future from corruption, manipulation, and division.

A powerful story comes to mind from a Sunday school class: the story of the Tower of Babel. It tells how humanity, at one point, was united in one language and one purpose—they wanted to reach God. Imagine that! They began to build a tower that would reach the heavens. But God saw what was happening and came down to confuse their language, scattering them across the earth so they could no longer understand one another. My point here is what was said in that true story: they were of **ONE MIND**, and that is the reason they were unstoppable. Nothing was impossible for them as long as they were united—one mind, one task, one mission.

And that is what we see today. Whether for good or for evil, when people are united, they gain tremendous power. Oh, that the countries of the world would have **strong leadership in ONE MIND**, one cause! That their greatest desire would be to seek the best for their citizens and for the generations yet to come. Lord, grant us that in the nations of the world.

Imagine a world where leaders are not driven by greed or personal ambition but by the sincere will to uplift their people; where decisions are made not for political gain but for moral good; where unity is not forced but born out of shared vision and compassion. Such nations would stand as beacons of hope, immune to corruption and manipulation. May we see that kind of unity rise again—a unity that builds, not destroys; that heals, not divides; that leads with strength, courage, and unwavering faith.

Chapter 10
Israel, Iran, Hamas, Russia and Others

As we write this chapter, hostages in the Middle East have begun to be released as part of Phase One of an agreement. We rejoice for those reunited with loved ones and mourn for those who have lost family members. The suffering caused by war is immeasurable, affecting innocent lives on all sides.

We believe that some hostages presumed dead may still be alive, and we pray for their safe return. Hope must never be abandoned.

Phase Two of the peace process, if achieved, will likely be temporary. History shows that peace in this region often lasts only for a season. Evil forces continue to use groups and governments to carry out acts of violence.

The lesson is clear: be prepared. Teach your children faith, love, and resilience. Guide them to trust in God and uphold truth, for the world they face will test them greatly.

We stand for the people on all sides—the innocent, the ones who speak out against wars, the peacemakers who refuse to let hatred define their hearts. Here is where we witness the true heart of the nations: some that stand boldly for evil and hate the good, and others that, blinded by pride or ideology, do not see the wrong they commit but instead pass the blame to others. It is in these moments of global conflict that the character of nations is revealed—not through their words, but through their actions, their compassion, and their willingness to defend truth over politics.

Yes, we pray for peace, but we know that peace will be temporary, not permanent. History teaches us that lasting peace does not come from treaties alone, but from transformed hearts. As mentioned in other chapters, we strongly believe that these moments of peace—if and when we experience them—are **moments of grace**, opportunities given to us to put our affairs in order. In such times, we are called to prepare ourselves for the challenges ahead, to strengthen our faith, our values, and our unity.

Mountain tops do not shape our character—the **valleys** do. It is in the hard times, the struggles, and the moments when hope seems distant that we are refined and made stronger. The mountain tops may bring us joy, but the valleys teach us endurance, humility, and wisdom. Those who only seek the mountaintop moments often fail to understand that true growth happens when we walk through the storms with faith and perseverance.

We have traveled to those regions—though we will not mention the countries—but some will understand what we are trying to say.

We were taken to a border between two nations that have been in conflict for generations, wars that seem to have no end. What I saw there deeply impacted me and confirmed my beliefs. On one side of the border, there were tall fences, layers of barbed wire, and stretches of sand so that guards could easily detect if anyone had crossed into their territory. There was vigilance, fear, and defense.

But my point here is this: the other side of the border had **no fences**, no sand to mark intrusions, no visible measures of fear. That was the day I realized who were the oppressors and who were the ones under attack most of the time. That simple contrast spoke volumes—one side living in constant suspicion, the other in quiet endurance. It is moments like these that make us pause and ask, "What have we been told? What have we chosen to believe?"

I share this story not to take sides but to awaken discernment. It should help people understand that we must do our research before deciding which side we support and which side we stand against— because we might, without knowing it, be supporting the wrong side. Truth is not always what the media portrays, nor what powerful voices insist upon. Sometimes, truth hides in the silent suffering of the innocent, in the quiet resilience of those who refuse to surrender their humanity even when the world forgets them.

IMAGINE, living all your life thinking you were right—and then finding out at the end that you were totally wrong. That realization would be heartbreaking, yet it is happening every day to those who follow ideologies without seeking truth.

That is one of the reasons for this book: to allow some and challenge most to seek truth **before** we endorse or support a group, a movement, or a cause. For truth is not a matter of opinion—it is absolute, unchanging, and divinely revealed.

Because if you believe in heaven, then understand this: there is only **ONE HEAVEN**—not two or three. Not one for the Democrats and another for the Republicans. Not one for the Blacks and one for the Whites. There is one heaven for those who have received the revelation of truth and have chosen **righteousness**, which means choosing what is right in the eyes of God. Righteousness is the path of right choice—the path that benefits not just one group, but all who seek what heaven has to offer.

And so, our message remains: stand for truth, even when it costs you; seek understanding before forming judgment; and remember that unity founded on righteousness will outlast every temporary peace this world can offer. When nations rise and fall, when ideologies shift and fade, only truth and love will endure.

Chapter 11
The Goal for Open Borders (To Get Votes)

The goal of open borders has always been political—primarily to secure more votes. Democrats understood that to win elections, they needed to increase their voter base, even if it meant bending or breaking the law. Many believe this strategy was evident in 2020 and became harder to execute in 2024, prompting a push to bring in as many new residents as possible.

But beyond the numbers and political maneuvering lies a deeper issue—one that touches the very soul of a nation. A government that prioritizes power over principle, votes over virtue, and control over compassion begins to lose its moral compass. The open-border agenda, under the banner of "humanitarian concern," has in many cases become a disguise for political gain. While the rhetoric emphasizes compassion, the results reveal chaos—communities overwhelmed, law enforcement stretched thin, and citizens struggling to be heard in their own land.

This disregard for national security and citizens' safety led to severe consequences: crimes, exploitation, and economic strain. It demonstrated a lack of care for the people who elected them. Providing illegal immigrants with free healthcare, licenses, and voting privileges undermines the foundation of democracy. When laws are selectively applied, and when citizenship is devalued to a mere political token, the integrity of a nation begins to erode. The very idea of equal rights and fair representation becomes clouded by manipulation and opportunism.

Citizens continue voting for leaders who harm them, driven by misinformation and loyalty to a party rather than logic or morality. The world watches this with disbelief. It is astonishing to witness how narratives are shaped and controlled—how truth becomes secondary to emotion, and facts are replaced by slogans. The people are promised hope, yet what they receive are policies that burden them, divide them, and diminish the nation's strength.

The solution is simple: focus on policies that benefit citizens, cooperate across party lines, and restore integrity to governance. Instead, Democrats doubled down on defending their mistakes, losing credibility and votes. Pride has blinded leadership from repentance. Rather than humbling themselves before the truth and seeking to correct the damage, they build higher walls of deception, blaming others for the results of their own failures.

The far left's influence now dominates their party, threatening national stability. Americans who understand history know socialism and communism never succeed—they destroy nations from within. Once embraced, these ideologies promise equality but deliver poverty, control, and despair. The pattern is clear throughout history: the more a government grows beyond its rightful limits, the less freedom remains for its people.

America stands at a crossroad—a defining moment where the choices made today will determine the fate of generations. The struggle is not merely political; it is moral and spiritual. The fight is not between red and blue states, but between truth and deception, between righteousness and corruption. The choice remains between **revival or ruin**. America's children are at stake.

To restore what has been lost, the nation must return to its founding principles: faith in God, respect for law, love for country, and care for fellow citizens. Borders are not built to keep compassion out—they are built to protect what is sacred within. A strong nation can still be a compassionate nation, but it must never trade security for sentiment, or truth for political advantage.

Blessed is the nation that makes the true God its God. Without that foundation, every policy, every election, and every border becomes meaningless. Only when righteousness leads the nation can freedom truly endure.

CHAPTER 12
A CALL TO SO-CALLED CHRISTIANS, BELIEVERS, AND RELIGIOUS

Just because someone calls themselves a Christian doesn't mean they live according to God's word. A true Christian stands for righteousness and reflects their faith in actions and choices.

It is shocking how many self-identified believers support parties or policies that contradict biblical principles, such as:

- Open borders
- Same-sex marriage
- Gender surgeries for minors
- Men in women's sports and bathrooms-
- Protecting illegal immigrants over citizens
- Supporting leaders who lie or attack authority instead of praying for them

and the list goes on and on.

Scripture teaches that judgment begins in the house of God. Many churches have lost reverence for God, placing politics above truth. The prayers of the righteous—not merely those who identify as

Christian—carry power. Righteousness means living in obedience and alignment with God's word.

It is hard to see so-called believers endorsing these evil practices and beliefs—protecting criminals, ignoring injustices, and allowing the very things mentioned above, as well as countless other harmful practices, to affect our children and young women. Even more troubling, many of us have accepted these things, turned a blind eye, and allowed what God clearly opposes to flourish in our midst.

Scripture warns us about such times. It tells us that we have become worse than Sodom and Gomorrah. If you are unfamiliar with that story, I encourage you to read it—you will understand the gravity of the times in which we are living. The corruption, immorality, and total disregard for righteousness were so severe in those cities that God destroyed them, sparing only the righteous who He allowed to escape. And make no mistake: the situation today is even worse in some ways. The warning is clear—when a society repeatedly rejects God's truth and embraces deception, destruction is never far behind.

Again, the reason we write this book is not to condemn for the sake of condemnation, but to help someone see the distinction between right and wrong. We want to guide both young and old in making the right choices, and to eliminate the deception that infiltrates our lives so that we might live in true freedom. Freedom is not merely the absence of oppression; it is the presence of truth, discernment, and alignment with God's will.

We are called to follow truth, not a man, a media network, or any organization that prioritizes influence over righteousness. Like the Bereans in the time of Paul and Silas, we must be diligent in our research, examining teachings, ideologies, and practices against the Word of God. Only then can we discern what is right and what is deception.

Do not be deceived. There is a way that seems right unto men, but the end of that way is death—without God, without truth, without righteousness. Many are walking paths that appear convenient, popular, or even logical, but these paths lead only to spiritual ruin. Recognize the danger. Reject the lie. Stand firmly in the truth that God has provided, and choose life—not just for yourself, but for those who look to you for guidance.

The choice is ours: to follow the crowd or to follow God, to accept deception or to seek understanding, to live in bondage or to embrace true freedom. May this book serve as a lamp to guide your steps, as a mirror to reveal the deception that surrounds us, and as a call to action—to live faithfully, wisely, and courageously in the times we are given.

CHAPTER 13
THE INSANITY OF SANCTUARY
CITIES

If harboring a criminal is illegal, how can sanctuary cities exist? These cities openly defy federal law by protecting illegal immigrants and providing them with benefits funded by taxpayers. It's a blatant contradiction of justice.

Mayors and governors who support such policies should be held accountable for breaking federal law. In most countries, they would face imprisonment for defying national authority. Yet in the USA, they continue unchecked, prioritizing political power over citizens' safety.

This undermines law enforcement agencies such as ICE and the FBI. The administration must act—arrest those violating their oaths and restore the rule of law. Protecting citizens must always come first.

It was shocking to see a clip from a recent debate in which Democratic candidates were asked a seemingly simple question: *"Would you continue to support undocumented immigrants?"* Every single candidate raised their hand in confirmation, and the crowd applauded.

This moment was significant because it appeared that these politicians were openly saying: *we will break the law, and we do not care what Americans—or the world—thinks. We will place undocumented immigrants ahead of citizens.* Yet, despite this public admission, no one has faced legal consequences.

The concern deepens when you consider that many of these same officials now publicly state that they will not support ICE or law enforcement in deporting criminals from their cities. Again, no government officials are charged or face prison time. In many other countries, politicians who openly defy the law in this way would face serious consequences. (In the country we were born in, these politicians would be in prison for defying their constitution and common sense.) The world is watching, waiting to see if the United States will ever enforce accountability. The hope is that it will, and soon, in order to send a strong message: government officials cannot openly defy the law without consequences.

Contrast this with situations involving ordinary citizens. If a teacher—or any individual—speaks vilely or rejoices at the death of someone, like Charlie Kirk, they are often fired immediately, without question. But politicians, even those who incite violence or express hatred toward citizens or groups based on their political stance, religion, or beliefs, appear to be immune from persecution. The world—and Americans—are waiting to see whether the United States will enforce justice against domestic threats that harm the wellbeing of its citizens and impose massive costs on the economy through security and litigation. These resources could instead be used for positive initiatives, like providing clean water in California or building homes for those who have lost theirs, rather than policing the hatred of officials who fail to serve their citizens.

A useful example to consider is El Salvador. Not long ago, it was one of the most dangerous countries in the world, plagued by daily murders and rampant gang control. Then, a new president was elected with overwhelming support—likely around 84% of the vote—who made bold reforms to fight crime and corruption. Today, El Salvador is considered one of the safest countries in the world, with reports of entire periods—such as 1,000 days—passing without a single murder. Corrupt politicians were jailed, and the president, despite being called a "dictator" and facing criticism similar to what leaders in the U.S. often face, transformed the nation. (A book on el Salvador and their president is coming out January 2026.)

The lesson here is clear: meaningful change is often met with resistance. People naturally resist change, especially when it challenges entrenched power structures or social ideologies. Yet, those willing to accept reforms for the betterment of society are the ones who ultimately benefit the most. Many Americans are facing similar choices today—some are resisting reforms because the agenda of certain leaders aligns with ideological goals rather than the practical needs of citizens.

Ultimately, the question remains: will U.S. leaders prioritize the wellbeing of their citizens, uphold the law, and address corruption, or will ideological agendas continue to take precedence over the safety and prosperity of the nation? The world is watching, and the answer will define the future of accountability and justice in America.

Chapter 14
A Word to the Stream Media: Power of Media to Deceive

The mainstream media's corruption has become a global embarrassment. Many networks perpetuate false narratives and cover-ups, manipulating viewers for profit and political influence.

Journalists have become propagandists, knowingly spreading misinformation. How could anyone be proud of such deceit? It raises moral questions—how can one work for or support a system built on lies?

The media's power to deceive is immense, shaping opinions and fueling division. Some people continue consuming these falsehoods because hatred clouds their judgment. The world watches in disbelief.

Lord, have mercy on this generation, and restore truth to communication.

The truth of the matter is that the so-called "woke" media has, in many ways, backfired on themselves. In trying to shape narratives and control public perception, they have exposed themselves to the world. It has become increasingly clear that much of what they say is not necessarily their own belief, but rather what they are instructed to say—likely because they have a job to protect and perhaps make a good living doing so.

Yet, the absurdity of some of the things they share has become obvious even to many of their followers. More and more people are waking up to the reality that these networks are not necessarily operating in the best interest of America. Instead, they are speaking primarily on behalf of the left, and in many cases, the far-left.

The truth is that America is not ready for a far-left government yet. The ideas and policies being promoted are extreme, and many citizens are not willing to accept them. Still, it is clear that efforts to push this agenda will continue, relentlessly, until they succeed. Why? Because the world is not getting better on its own. We are witnessing events and societal changes that are unprecedented, things we have never seen before.

This is why we believe we are living in a unique season—a season of grace, mixed with judgment. Judgment? Yes. Look around you. Observe what people truly believe in. Some are paid to appear as though they support certain ideas, but many genuinely accept the nonsense being promoted. The ideas we address in this book are real, and they matter because they shape the future of our society.

We want everyone to hear us clearly when we say this is a season of grace. It is a time to act, to prepare, to strengthen yourself and your loved ones. This season might last only months, perhaps a few years—but whatever the length, we must use it wisely. We must prepare for what is coming, even though we cannot know exactly what that will look like. One thing is certain: the world is not on a path toward becoming a better place. For many, the world is already facing unprecedented challenges.

So, we urge you to enjoy this season while it lasts. But do so with purpose. Fight on your knees in prayer, fight with your voice, and fight for your children and future generations. Let us leave a legacy that protects them, and a legacy that ensures there will be people in the world who can rise, make history, and make a real difference. Even if the world becomes darker and more challenging than what we face today, we must remember this principle: *we can still shine our light in the midst of darkness.*

Let us shine with truth. Let us shine with love—for our people, for our country. Let us go down in history as those who fought for what was right, who stood firm in the face of adversity, and who made a meaningful difference in the world. Our actions today will shape the legacy we leave behind.

CHAPTER 15
CREATING A DEPARTMENT TO HANDLE FACT CHECKING (FACT CHECK GOVERNMENT DEPARTMENT)

Both political parties desire to control the spread of misinformation in the media, yet freedom of speech makes it difficult to regulate. False information divides the nation and has led to unrest, violence, and even murder.

The question remains: how can this be fixed? People rely on biased media sources instead of doing their own research, creating deep division across the country. This pattern is visible not only in politics but in religion and social life as well.

One possible solution:

- Establish a government committee to fact-check false information broadcast publicly. This would apply to both Democrats and Republicans. The committee's goal would be to protect the USA from rhetoric that incites hate or violence, not to restrict free speech.

- Those spreading lies should face public accountability. If their statements are verified as false, they should be corrected publicly. Accountability would foster responsibility and reduce harmful rhetoric.

Such measures could help restore national unity and rebuild trust between citizens, government, and the media.

This branch of government could serve as a vital check—a department that minimizes the spread of harmful, baseless rhetoric. When people know their words have consequences, they would likely think twice before spreading claims or statements that have no foundation but still carry the potential to ignite hatred and violence. Words have power. Misused, they can lead to unrest, riots, and billions of dollars spent on security and damage control—resources that could otherwise be invested in prevention, education, and community support.

You might argue that the government is already addressing these issues, but the results speak for themselves. Despite efforts, we continue to witness leaders, governors, mayors, and other politicians making incendiary statements without facing any legal consequences. As we write this book, nobody has gone to jail for openly defying the law in this way—but we believe that time is coming. Accountability is inevitable.

The United States has fought wars overseas, defending freedom and justice on foreign soil, but now it is time to confront the growing threats and corruption within its own borders. We are seeing the beginnings of this internal reckoning, yet we also witness fierce opposition from those who resist doing what is good for the country.

Law enforcement must rise to the challenge. Officers must uphold their duty to protect and serve, rather than yielding to the pressures of the far-left political agenda. If a law enforcement officer finds that they cannot perform their job properly due to political interference, they must have the courage to speak out or resign, even at personal cost. There will always be other states and communities willing to welcome those who stand firm for justice and integrity.

The United States may seem divided, but there are millions of citizens who firmly support law, order, and accountability. The nation's survival—and the safety of its people—depends on those principles. We pray for mercy upon the United States and for countries around the world, that leaders and citizens alike may act with wisdom, courage, and righteousness in these turbulent times.

Chapter 16
"False Rhetoric" Leads to Violence

In modern societies, words can be as dangerous as weapons. Public discourse shapes beliefs, influences behavior, and sets the stage for collective action. When rhetoric becomes false or intentionally misleading, it can destabilize entire communities.

False rhetoric is among the most dangerous threats facing any democracy. It spreads division, fuels hatred, and can lead directly to acts of violence. False narratives, repeated over time, normalize extreme behavior, making aggression seem acceptable. Freedom of speech should not be an excuse for language that incites harm. Politicians and media figures must recognize that reckless speech has consequences. Their words can legitimize prejudice, embolden extremists, and sow mistrust between citizens and government institutions.

In recent years, we have seen violent attacks inspired by rhetoric that dehumanizes others—language labeling opponents as fascists, Nazis, or traitors. These labels are not mere metaphors; they serve to vilify entire groups, reducing empathy and creating an "us versus them" mentality. Studies of radicalization show that repeated exposure to such rhetoric can tip unstable individuals toward violent action, especially when reinforced by online echo chambers and social networks that amplify extremist content.

The USA must pass laws holding individuals accountable for rhetoric that leads to violence. Legal frameworks in some European countries already set precedents for prosecuting incitement without undermining legitimate free speech. False rhetoric can radicalize unstable individuals, pushing them to harm innocent people. El Salvador's success in restoring law and order shows that decisive leadership can reverse chaos. Likewise, the USA must act decisively to protect its citizens. Evil grows when good people remain silent. Communities, civic leaders, and ordinary citizens must speak out against inflammatory speech to prevent its normalization. The world is watching how America handles this moment.

A government department dedicated to identifying and penalizing false rhetoric could prevent hate-fueled crimes. Such a body could track online and offline communication patterns, issue warnings, and work with law enforcement to intervene before rhetoric turns into action. Accountability would strengthen democracy, not weaken it. Citizens must support policies that defend truth and stability, ensuring a safer nation for future generations. Educational programs that teach media literacy, critical thinking, and civic responsibility would complement these measures, making society less vulnerable to manipulation.

CHAPTER 17
DEMOCRATS SEEM LIKE THEY'RE FROM ANOTHER PLANET: SUPPORTING ILLEGAL

Political decisions increasingly appear disconnected from the realities that ordinary citizens face. Policy choices that affect national security, immigration, and law enforcement are often debated in abstract terms, leaving the general public unsure of their implications.

We are witnessing behavior that defies logic—political decisions that seem detached from reality. Many Americans vote without understanding the policies they support. This blind loyalty divides families and destroys communities. Patterns of voting influenced more by tradition or emotion than informed judgment reveal a troubling trend: policy literacy is often secondary to party loyalty or identity politics.

Common voting patterns reveal emotional rather than informed decisions:

- Voting based on ethnicity or tradition rather than policy.

- Supporting a candidate because of appearance or party history.
- Trusting biased media sources instead of conducting independent research.

Politicians exploit these tendencies, offering free incentives instead of real solutions. Incentives that appear generous in the short term may undermine long-term economic stability or public safety, leaving communities exposed to consequences they did not anticipate. The result is chaos—citizens supporting those who harm them, and corrupt leaders remaining in power. This disconnect between rhetoric and reality erodes trust in democratic institutions, making reform more difficult over time.

The world is astonished to see Americans voting for officials who protect criminals instead of citizens, and for judges who block justice because of personal bias. The USA must wake up. Those who use public office to destroy the nation should face imprisonment for abuse of power. Ensuring that the judiciary and law enforcement uphold the law impartially is essential; without accountability, corruption and favoritism flourish. The Supreme Court, once a symbol of fairness, must restore its reputation by ensuring justice. Corrupt judges and politicians should be exposed and punished, setting a global example of accountability and moral leadership.

Civic engagement is essential to reverse this trend. Voters must be encouraged to research policies, assess real-world impacts, and challenge leaders who misrepresent facts for political gain. Grassroots movements, watchdog organizations, and independent media all play a critical role in empowering citizens to make informed decisions. Immigration and security policies must be practical, enforceable, and aligned with national interest, balancing compassion with responsibility. Only through informed participation can democracy protect both citizens and the integrity of public institutions.

CHAPTER 18
CRIMINALS RELEASED FROM PRISON TO MURDER SOMEONE

The greatest crime is not only committed by criminals but by those in power who release them. It is a betrayal of the public trust, a deliberate act that turns the machinery of justice into a weapon against the very people it was meant to protect. When decision-makers prioritize convenience or politics over justice, the ripple effects devastate entire communities. Neighborhoods once considered safe become zones of fear, schools and workplaces are disrupted, and the psychological scars linger long after the immediate crime has passed. Many individuals who should have remained imprisoned or been deported were set free, only to commit rape, robbery, and murder. These are not mere numbers in a report; each case is a shattered life, a family torn apart, a community left questioning the very foundations of law and order. Each act of violence could have been prevented had the proper systems and accountability measures been enforced. Checks and balances, when ignored, cease to function, allowing human lives to be treated as expendable in the pursuit of expediency.

The pain endured by families of victims is unimaginable. Grief lingers for years, affecting not just parents and siblings, but neighborhoods and social structures as well. Children grow up with the absence of parents, friends live with fear, and the sense of safety in one's own community erodes with each preventable tragedy. These tragedies were preventable. Politicians and judges responsible for such decisions bear the blame for enabling these crimes. By failing to act with integrity, they create a culture where human life is devalued, and justice is negotiable. Their choices reflect a systemic failure, where laws are manipulated rather than upheld, eroding public trust. Citizens begin to question whether the institutions meant to protect them are instead complicit in their harm. Their actions prioritized political gain over public safety, trading justice for votes. In this exchange, the currency is human suffering—a cost too high to ignore. And yet, history shows that those in power often continue to gamble with lives for personal advancement.

The world is watching as corruption is exposed. Global scrutiny highlights that this is not a localized problem but a symptom of broader governance failures. From international news outlets to human rights organizations, eyes are fixed on nations that allow political expediency to override morality and law. Officials who lied about border security and released dangerous individuals must face justice. No rhetoric, no spin, no obfuscation can undo the real, measurable harm caused by these decisions. Transparency and accountability are not optional—they are the backbone of a functioning democracy. Their deceit insulted the intelligence of the American people and cost innocent lives. Every statistic represents a story, a life altered or lost, and a societal wound that will take generations to heal. Every unpunished betrayal leaves a legacy of mistrust that corrodes society from within.

Ultimately, judgment—both moral and divine—awaits those who betrayed their duty. No amount of political maneuvering can shield one from the consequences of deliberate negligence. Time exposes all deceit, and history remembers the choices made at moments of moral testing. Even religious leaders complicit in these lies will face accountability. Faith and authority carry responsibility; when misused, they amplify harm instead of offering guidance. Their silence or complicity is not a neutral act; it is an endorsement of injustice, a signal to others that power can operate without consequence. The time has come for truth to prevail. Only by confronting uncomfortable realities can a society rebuild justice and restore faith in its institutions. Without courage and collective demand for integrity, corruption will continue to thrive, leaving society fractured and vulnerable.

May God have mercy on us all. And may we, as a nation and as individuals, awaken to our responsibility to demand integrity, protect the innocent, and never remain silent in the face of wrongdoing.

CHAPTER 19
THE LEFT AND FAR LEFT NEVER THOUGHT TRUMP WOULD HAVE THE POWER HOUSE AGAIN

The left never believed Donald Trump would regain the White House. Convinced of their lasting control, they acted with impunity, assuming power would never change hands. They built strategies, narratives, and policies around the idea that their dominance was permanent. Social, cultural, and economic agendas were advanced with little regard for dissent, and opposition voices were often silenced, marginalized, or dismissed as irrelevant. The media, long an extension of partisan influence, amplified these narratives, shaping perception and fostering a sense of inevitability among the ruling elite. But in November 2024, the people proved them wrong. The election results shattered assumptions and upended expectations, revealing a disconnect between the governing class and the nation it purported to serve.

Now fear grips those who once manipulated the system with confidence. The tables have turned. Investigations into years of corruption are underway, exposing networks of influence, misuse of taxpayer funds, and systematic attempts to sway elections. Secret communications, financial misdeeds, and covert political maneuverings are being brought into the light. The hunted have become the hunters. High-ranking officials, corporate lobbyists, media figures, and even academic institutions that once operated above accountability are now scrutinized under the weight of the law. Justice demands exposure of deceit—from government agencies to media organizations complicit in spreading lies, misinformation, and partisan propaganda.

The coming years will reveal the true depth and breadth of political corruption, extending far beyond what most citizens imagined. Numerous officials who abused their offices, entrusted with the nation's welfare, will face charges, legal battles, and, in some cases, imprisonment. Trials will uncover hidden alliances, financial improprieties, and deliberate efforts to undermine democratic processes. These revelations will shake the foundations of public trust, forcing a reckoning with the institutions many assumed were infallible. What some call retribution, others see as a necessary cleansing, a reckoning that cannot be avoided if democracy is to endure.

The social and cultural consequences are equally profound. Citizens, long accustomed to partisan narratives and institutional secrecy, are awakening to the reality that power is not permanent and that accountability is inevitable. Grassroots movements, previously dismissed as fringe or extremist, gain legitimacy as the populace witnesses the consequences of unchallenged corruption. The public dialogue shifts from idle partisanship to a focus on transparency, reform, and civic responsibility. The lessons are stark: those entrusted with leadership must answer to the people, not to entrenched interests.

The world observes too, with a mixture of apprehension, fascination, and hope. Nations that once questioned the stability of American democracy are now witnessing the consequences of unchecked power. Allies and adversaries alike take note of the unfolding events, understanding that democratic accountability is not a weakness but a measure of national resilience. The unfolding investigations, trials, and political shifts serve as a reminder that no individual, party, or institution is immune to scrutiny. History is being rewritten—not by rhetoric, ideology, or public relations, but by evidence, action, and the undeniable will of the people.

Amid the uncertainty, there is a renewed sense of possibility. Citizens and institutions alike must grapple with a harsh truth: democracy is fragile, and vigilance is essential. The coming years will test the nation's commitment to justice, transparency, and rule of law. The exposure of deceit, the unmasking of corruption, and the pursuit of accountability will shape the political and cultural landscape for generations. The struggle between power and principle, between deception and truth, is far from over—but for the first time in decades, the scales are beginning to tip.

CHAPTER 20
THE INSANITY OF TAPPING
OFFICIALS' PHONES

The exposure of illegal surveillance on political officials marks a dark chapter in American history. What was once whispered in the corridors of power is now laid bare: government resources, meant to serve the people, were weaponized against them. Previous administrations, believing themselves untouchable, systematically monitored opponents, gathering private communications, emails, and phone calls with the intent to discredit, manipulate, and control. The scale of the operation revealed a level of hubris and audacity that stunned even the most seasoned political observers.

These actions were not mere missteps—they were deliberate assaults on democracy itself. By exploiting the machinery of the state for partisan advantage, these officials betrayed the foundational principles of transparency, fairness, and the rule of law. Citizens, who entrust their leaders with the immense power of governance, were treated as pawns in a game of political dominance. Trust was shattered, and confidence in institutions meant to safeguard liberty was eroded.

Yet, as history teaches, one reaps what one sows. The very forces that relied on deceit, manipulation, and clandestine operations are now facing accountability. Investigations have uncovered not only the scope of surveillance but also the coordination required to carry it out—an organized network of complicit actors spanning government agencies, contractors, and even media intermediaries. The revelation has sent shockwaves through Washington, with former officials, advisers, and operatives forced to confront evidence of their wrongdoing.

The next several years will bring consequences for those responsible. Legal proceedings, congressional hearings, and independent investigations will hold perpetrators to account. Citizens demand justice—not vengeance, but accountability—to ensure such abuses never recur. This is about more than punishing the guilty; it is about restoring faith in the system and reaffirming the principle that no one is above the law.

The future belongs to transparency, truth, and the restoration of lawful governance. Surveillance, coercion, and manipulation cannot define the American political system any longer. As the nation watches these proceedings unfold, a clear message emerges: the misuse of power has consequences, and the American people will not tolerate violations of their rights or betrayals of their trust.

Democracy, though tested, is resilient. It can be repaired, strengthened, and renewed—but only through vigilance, accountability, and an unwavering commitment to the principles that make it worth defending.

The insanity of tapping officials' phones serves as both a cautionary tale and a turning point. For too long, secrecy masked corruption, and fear stifled dissent. Now, sunlight is pouring into the dark corners of government. History will remember this period not merely for the scandal, but for the reckoning it provoked—a reminder that liberty, once endangered, can always be reclaimed by those brave enough to insist on the truth.

CHAPTER 21
SOCIALISM/COMMUNISM

For decades, the USA and its allies have fought communism and socialism. Yet these ideologies are now resurfacing, threatening to infiltrate American society. Nations such as Cuba and Venezuela serve as stark reminders of the devastation such systems bring.

Socialism promises equality but delivers oppression. It seduces with free benefits, then traps citizens under authoritarian control. Like an addict drawn to false comfort, societies under socialism lose freedom and prosperity.

The world prays that America resists this deception. Freedom requires vigilance, and the lessons of history must not be ignored. Encouragingly, there is hope—change is coming. Countries once trapped under oppressive regimes will soon experience liberty. The USA and the global community must support this awakening.

May the nations that have suffered under tyranny rise again, and may freedom reign where oppression once ruled.

The United States is truly blessed to have an administration committed to confronting socialism and exposing the dangers it brings. This administration stands as a bulwark against policies and ideologies that, throughout history, have eroded freedom, stifled innovation, and weakened nations from within. We believe that the present leadership represents one of the most consequential and positive developments in the nation's recent history. The proof lies not in rhetoric but in action—through the investigations, reforms, and exposures that are revealing the extent to which the left and far-left have undermined American institutions, policies, and values over the years.

No government is perfect, and no administration can claim absolute virtue. Yet, what the United States enjoys at this moment—a steadfast commitment to accountability, transparency, and the preservation of liberty—is the envy of many around the world. Nations that struggle under oppressive systems or bureaucratic stagnation often look to America with admiration, even as they recognize the ongoing internal struggles that the country faces. The current administration's efforts to confront corruption, challenge entrenched interests, and restore trust in governance are creating a model that countless people globally can aspire to but rarely experience.

We understand that the truths presented in this book may upset some readers. It is not intended to comfort, appease, or validate existing beliefs. Instead, its purpose is to provide a clear-eyed view of the United States from the perspective of an outsider looking in—a perspective that may be uncomfortable but is grounded in observation, evidence, and reflection. The realities revealed here, though unsettling, highlight the resilience and potential of the nation when guided by principled leadership.

As the philosopher Plato once wisely said, "No one is more hated than he that speaks truth." This observation resonates profoundly here. Speaking truth often challenges long-held assumptions, unsettles the comfortable, and provokes resistance. Yet, it is through truth—unflinching, uncompromising, and courageous—that societies grow, evolve, and correct their course. The United States, at this moment in history, is engaging in precisely that process: facing uncomfortable truths, confronting past mistakes, and striving to emerge stronger, freer, and more just than ever before.

This is not merely political commentary; it is a recognition of the unique moment in which the nation stands. The struggles, revelations, and reforms we witness today are shaping the future of America—not just for its citizens, but as a signal to the world of what democracy, liberty, and accountability can achieve when they are defended with courage and clarity.

CHAPTER 22
THE CHILDREN

As we approach the conclusion of this work, it is natural to reflect on the purpose of all we have written. Every chapter, every argument, every cautionary note has been in service of something far greater than ourselves: the well-being of the most vulnerable among us. There are few responsibilities as sacred as nurturing and protecting the next generation. We have left this topic for last because it is the most important one—our children. Throughout this book, we have mentioned them, but it is vital to dedicate a chapter solely to them: those who are lost, those being abused, those needing to be reunited with their families. Our prayers go out to their parents and to the law enforcement officers searching for them.

The Bible offers clear guidance on the value and protection of children:

- Matthew 18:6
- Matthew 19:13–15

We recommend watching The Sound of Freedom, a powerful film based on true events that expose the horrors of child trafficking.

The world's children are under attack, and many have turned a blind eye to their suffering. Those who ignore these crimes share in the guilt.

We praise the current administration (2025) for taking strong action to find missing children and reverse destructive policies. However, the work must continue. The attacks on education and morality are real and visible. Parents and teachers must stand for truth and protect the innocence of children.

We believe, as the majority of the world does, that there are only two genders—male and female. At birth, doctors declare, "It's a boy" or "It's a girl." This simple truth reflects divine order and creation. To deny it is to deny reality.

History reminds us: "Do not complain about what you have allowed." If we remain silent in the face of evil, we become participants in it. The world needs courageous voices willing to stand for truth, even when unpopular. Lord, protect our children, grandchildren, and all generations to come. May Your mercy and justice prevail. As we close this chapter, let it be a call to action as much as a reflection. Protecting children is not merely a duty for parents or policymakers; it is a responsibility for every one of us. We cannot afford complacency. Whether through prayer, vigilance, advocacy, or direct intervention, each of us has a role in safeguarding the innocent. Let this final chapter serve as both a warning and a beacon of hope. The battle for our children is ongoing, but with unwavering faith and courage, their future can be brighter.

www.ingramcontent.com/pod-product-compliance
Lightning Source LLC
Chambersburg PA
CBHW051226120626
46547CB00013B/1527